The underground imperial guards of 2200 years ago The Terra－cotta Army in the Mausoleum of Qin Shihuang

Edited by The Terra－cotta Army Museum

Chief editor Yuan Zhongyi
Associate Chief editor Lei Yuping Wu Yongqi
Zhang Zhongli Xu Weimin

Published by Cultural Relics Publishing House
Beijing, 1999

The Colorful plate of the Terra-cotta Army

The Artistic Reproduction of the Battle Formation
in Qin Dynasty ·· Yuan Zhongyi   *1*

Content

The Artistic Reproduction
of the Battle Formation in Qin Dynasty

Yuan ZhongYi

Qin Shihuang(259 BC to 210 BC)was the first feudal emperor in the history of the unified China. His large mausoleum is six kilometers to the east of Lin Tong District, Xi' an City. Ever since the sacrificial terra − cotta horses and warriors were unearthed in 1974, Pit 1, 2 and 3 have been discovered. In the three Pits, there are about 8000 lifesize pottery horses and human figures including chariot warriors, cavalry, infantry and other army branches. They are arranged in good order and look like a massive underground imperial army. Bearing different portraits and vivid expressions, the figurines are a bright pearl in the sculpture history of ancient China. Commonly loved by people in the world, the Terra − cotta Army of the Tomb of Emperor Qin has become known as the Eighth Wonder of the World, one of the great discoveries in the archaeology history in the 20st century. Together with the tomb, the Terra − cotta Army was enrolled into the list of world cultural heritage by the UNESCO(United Nations Educational, Scientific and Cultural Organization). It has become the valuable cultural property of not only the Chinese people, but also the whole human beings. To protect effectively the historic relic. the Terra − cotta Army Museum was established in 1979.

1. The discovery and excavation of the Terra − cotta Army

Pits of pottery warriors and horses are 1.5 kilometers to the east of the emperor's tomb. Before the land lied waste, nobody could imagine that there was an artistic treasure − house under the ground.

In March 1974, local farmers digging a well discovered some broken pieces of pottery

1

figures without knowing what they were. Later, after one year of exploration and tentative excavation, archaeologists confirmed that it was a large – scale pit – pit 1. The 14260 – square – meter Pit is 230 meters from east to west, 62 meters wide from north to south and 4.5 to 6.5 meters from the present ground. Calculating the arrangement density of the unearthed horses and warriors, archaeologists believed that there are about 6000 such figures and a large number of bronze arms. in Pit 1.

After the discovery of Pit 1, archaeologists kept exploring in the nearby area. On April23, 1976. Pit 2situated 20 meters northeast of Pit 1 was discovered, Pit 2 looks like a carpenter's square. the 6000 – square – meter Pit is 124 meters long from east to west, 98 meters wide from north to south and about 5 meters from the present ground. Inferring from the unearthed part, Pit 2 contains about 1, 300 pottery horses and warriors. Comparing with the content of Pit 1, Pit 2 comprises richer objects, including kneeling and standing warriors, cavalry and more than 80 chariots. Pit 2 is the essence of the Terra – cotta Army.

On May 11, 1976, archaeologists discovered Pit 3 situated 25 metres northwest of Pit 1. Pit 3 is smaller and irregular. Its plan is gravure and with a slop in the east. It is 28.8 meters long from east to west and 24.57 meters wide from north to south. The 520 – square – meter pit is 5.2 to 5.4 meters from the ground. In Pit 3 there are 72 pottery horses and warriors. Though it's smaller, Pit 3 is of great significance because it is in command of Pit 1 and 2. Pit 3 was named"Military Governmemt" in the ancient.

In summer in 1976, unfinished Pit 4 was discovered to the north of the middle of Pit 1 and between Pit 2 and 3. The 3600 – square – meter pit is rectangular. It is 48 meters long from east to west, 75 meters wide from north to south and 4.8 meters from the ground. There is no relics in Pit 4 because the project was forced to stop by the uprising farmers who occupied the area near the Terra – cotta Army at the end of Qin Dynasty (209BC) since Pit 4 is unfinished, people often ignore it when they count the pits.

Formerly Pit 1, 2, 3 and the unfinished Pit 4 were in one group. According to the ancient battle formation, Pit 1 is the right army and Pit 2 is the left. the unfinished Vault 4 is the recommended middle army and Pit 3 is the command post. Thus the four Pits form a complete battle formation system. It symbolizes the army defending Qin Shihuang's capital, which was named"guarding army"at that time.

It is a large tunnel building made of earth and wood. Specifically, first dig a 5 – meter – deep pit, in which parallel earth partitions are built, then arrange along the partitions wooden pillars with crossbeams on the top. Next place timbers across crossbeams and the partitions to form a shed, which is covered with reed mats. Finally spread earth over the mats and finish the top of the tunnel. At that time the top was about 2 meters above the ground and looked like a mound with a flat roof. The ground in the tunnel is paved with bricks and the room is 3.2 meters high. After arranging the pottery horses and warriors inside, the door is sealed up and the undergronnd vault becomes closed.

The Terra－cotta Army of the Tomb of Qin Shihuang is not recorded in literature. However, in the past 2000 years, people have constantly discovered broken pieces of pottery horses and warriors. In addition, on the pits, people have discovered six tombs built in the Eastern Han Dynasty (25 AD to 220AD), over 20 modern and contemporary tombs, three wells and disturbing pits. In these tombs and pits, broken pieces of pottery figures were unearthed, but then nobody knew that they were precious relics. On the contrary, the pieces were mistaken as ominous monsters. As a consequence, people paid little attention to them at all. The mysterious veil on the Terra－cotta Army was not removed until archaeologists participated in after local farmer digging a well discovered the pit. Moreover, until then did the Terra－corra Army have the chance to display its amazing demeanour to the world.

In the 25 years after 1974, the exploration and excavation of the vaults have never stopped. By now, one third of Pit 1 and the whole Pit 3 have been unearthed. Pit 2 is being excavated now. People have unearthed over 2000 pottery horses and warriors and more than 40000 various bronze weapons. In October, 1979, the Terra－cotta Army Relic Museum was established. It opens to the public while excavation continues. People could not only appreciate the unearthed pottery horses and warriors, but also obtain new information about the unearthing process of relics and knowledge related to archaeological excavation. People can always find something new here and they love it .

2.Classification and arrangement of the Terra－cotta Army

(1)Classification of the Terra－cotta Army.

Qin is a well－known powerful military country with thousands of chariots, tens of thousands of horses and millions of infantrymen. Depending on the strong army, Qin shihuang annexed the territories of dukes or princes and unitied the whole China. The Terra－cotta Army is the miniature of the Qin Army and it is also divided into chariots, infantrymen and cavalrymen.

1.Chariots.

There are more than 130 chariots in Pit 1, 2 and 3. Made of wood, these chariots have rotten when unearthed and only relics remain. Each chariot has two 1.35 − meter − high wheels, one shaft and four pottery horses harnessing in the front. The horizontal rectangular carriage is 1.4 meters wide and 1.2 meters long from front to back. Arround the carriage there are 40 − centimeter − high lattice railings with an open door in the back. The chariots are painted and some have colored drawings or patterns on. With complete driving implements, these chariots are the same as those used in the battle field.

The chariots in the pits can be subdivided into the commanding ones and the ordinary ones. The black commanding chariots have magnificent ornaments and exquisite designs. Above the chariots there are round canopies and bells and drums hang. On the chariot there are three pottery human figures with different duties: one is the general; one is the driver and another is "Chariot Right". The general is in charge of bells and drums and he orders the army to advance or withdraw. In other words, "the warriors advance when they hear the drums and fight when drums are heavily beaten. As soon as they hear bells ring, they should stop fighting and withdraw when bells are heavily beaten. ("Wei Liao Zi"). The driver drives the chariot and makes sure that it moves forward and backforward freely and safely. As to "Chariot Right", he is responsible for protecting the general and pushing the chariot when the road is muddy or dangerous. As a matter of fact, "Chariot Right" has to be strong and tough.

The ordinary chariots are for warriors and each has three pottery figures, too: the driver, "Chariot Left" and "Chariot Right". The driver stands in the middle; "Chariot Left" stands on the left and "Chariot Right" on the right. They stand in a row. In ancient times, warriors can only stand on the chariot. The driver drives horses. "Chariot Left" and "Chariot Right" fight against enemies with pikes, ge, arrows and crossbows. If enemies are far, they shoot arrows. Otherwise, they stab them with pikes and ge. The three warriors all have suits of armour on. The driver's arms stretch forward and his hands hold reins tightly. "Chariot Left" and "Chariot Right" hold weapons in one hand and the other hand hold reins. Their expression and gesture are quite vivid.

2.Cavalrymen.

In Pit 2, 116 pottery cavalrymen are unearthed. The lifesize pottery horses are 2 meters long and 1.72 meters tall. On the back of the horse is the saddle and its head wears the bridle and reins. There is a cavalryman standing in front of each horse. He holds reins in one hand and crossbows in the other. The horse and cavalryman are lifelike. Four horses form one group and three groups stand in the same Line. Thus Lines of horses make up a rectangular file. The horses and cavalrymen are full of power and grandeur and they display vividly the Qin cavalry to the public.

The Qin cavalry first came into being in the 7th BC, and it developed into an independent and powerful armed branch in Qin Dynasty. The cavalry is spry and light, so it is often ordered to attack the enemy all of a sudden, disturb and chase the defeated enemies.

3. Infantrymen.

There are about 7,000 pottery infantrymen in the pits and the number is larger than that of chariots and cavalrymen. Based on their ranks, infantrymen contain officers and ordinary warriors. Officers are subdivided into high — ranking (commonly known as "generals"), middle — ranking and low — ranking ones. Ordinary warriors are distinguished as those with light packs and those with heavy packs. The differences between the pottery figures mentioned above lie in their clothes, ornaments, armors and hats.

The high — ranking officers wear double long coats covered with colored scale armors and hats and hats shaped like cockscombs Hands of some officers hang in front·of their abdomens and lean on long swords. Arms of others hang naturally. They hold their heads high and have an impressive bearing. You can infer that they are high — ranking military officers from just one glance.

The middle — ranking officers wear double — board long hats and suits of armor. There are two different kinds of armor coat. One is the chest armor with colored design which can only protect the front part of the body. The other is a coat with bigger shell pieces and colored edge. Some figures hold swords in their hands and stand with an awe — inspiring manner. Some stand beside the general and look like his assistant. Others stand among soldiers. They are dashing, spirited and they have great stature.

Low — ranking officers wear single — board long hats. Some who are not dressed in suits of armor have light packs. Others wear armors without colored design on the coat . They have swords in one hand and pikes, ge or other weapons in the other.

Warriors with light packs do not wear armors or helmets. They have leggings on and hold crossbows in their hands. Most of infantrymen with light packs stand in the front of the formation because it is necessary for vanguard to be brisk, wise, brave and good at marching. In ancient battles , enemies couldn't be defeated unless the vanguard was sharp.

All the warriors with heavy packs wear armors, so they are also called armoured warriors. There are more armoured than other warriors in Pit 1, 2 and 3 and the number is about 80% of infantrymen. Armoured warriors can be divided into many different types. According to their postures, there are archers shooting on their kneels, on their feet and those standing on their splayfeet. According to their dress, some warriors have round hair worn in a bun on their heads, some have flat hair with six plaits, some wear conical hats (named jieze in ancient times) some hold bows and crossbows in their hands. Others hold dagger – axes, pikes, bo and other various weapons. The differences result from their different positions and responsibilities in the battle formation

In China, early infantrymen had no independent establishment. During Shang, Zhou, the Spring and Autumn Period, chariots played an important role in battles. At that time , infantrymen belonged to chariots. In each chariot, there are 10 infantrymen, who fought in with the chariot. In the Warring States Period (4th century BC – 3rd centurg BC) besides the dependent infantrymen, independent ones appeared and the whole army was made up of chariots, infantry and calvary, the three independent units. In the pits, there are all the three units and infantrymen can be distinguished ones and independent ones. Therefore the pits are a portrayal true to the ancient army establishment.

(2) The battle formation of the Terra – cotta Army.

In battles, ancient warriors stand in a certain formation, which is named battle formation.

About 6000 pottery horses and warriors in Pit 1 form a large rectangular battle formation. The way to arrange them is as following: There is a horizontal team made up of three lines of warriors with light packs in the front of formation. In each line there are 68 figures and altogether there are 204. This is the vanguard of the formation. The body of formation is after vanguard, which includes 38 files of chariots alternating with infantry. Two wings formed of two lines of infantrymen are on the right and left of the formation. The warriors all face outside to fight enemies from the two sides. At the back is the rearguard made up of three lines of infantrymen. They are responsible for beating enemies from the back. In short, we can see how tight the arrangement is.

The formation in Pit 2 looks like the carpenter's square and it includes four smaller formations. The kneeling and standing archers in Formation 1 are in the front. The kneeling archers are in the middle and the standing ones surround them. Formation 2 is on the right and comprises 64 chariots. In the middle is the rectangular Formation 3 which includes chariots, infantry and cavalry. The rectangular Formation 4 is on the left and there are 108 cavalrymen in it. The above four smaller formations compose an organic big formation with various combat branches. Each small formation can fight independently and all of them is an integrated mass. In this way, the big formation utilizes the power of different combat branches fighting in coordination.

In Pit 3 there is one commanding chariot and 64 infantrymen with ritual bronze weapons in their hands, They stand face to face along a narrow lane and they are on heavy guard. In Pit 3, people also unearthed antlers and rotten animal bones used as sacrifice and in practising divination. In old times, before the army set out to fight, they practised divination and prayed to their ancestors and deities to get their bless and win. Pit 3 is the post commanding Pit 1 and 2.

The arrangement of 8000 pottery horses and warriors is a vivid picture of the ancient battle formation. Being grand and of great momentum, it is a lively reproduction of the glorious Qin Army.

3. The artistic style and making techniques of the Terra − cotta Army

People's first impression of the Terra − cotta Army is that the figures are tall, numerous and lifelike. They reveal a magnanimous manner and tremendous force. They also shock people and present strong artistic charm.

The realistic − style Terra − cotta Army imitates real objects and tries to be similar. On the whole, it simulates the arrangement of chaviots, cavalry and infantry in the Qin Army. Meanwhile it is the reproduction of Qin army's strong soldiers, sturdy horses and ever − victorious results in battles. It reflects the characteristics of that period and it is a large − scale memorial sculpture group. Simulating the real clothes, weapons and the driving equipment, the pottery ones are a mirror of the real social life. Even some details stem from reality. For example, wrinkles on the foreheads of all high − ranking officers indicate that they are weather − beaten and battle − tested. This is in accordance with the officer − selecting principle in Qin Dynasty. Specifically, the first standard is their martial arts. If their martial arts are on similar levels, officers are chosen according to their ages and morality. Real people and horses are prototypes of the pottery ones, so they are different in appearance and their characteristics are distinct. This makes audience feel intimate. The Terra − cotta Army is a typical successful example of the ancient realistic art.

The Qin people upheld forces and they advocated fighting bravely in battles. In their value, people who had military accomplishments were honorable. This idea is embodied in plastic arts and people pursue mental and physical beauty, which is the coordination of power and bravery. Under the influence of this view, the fundamental characteristics of the pottery figures are: the central axles are cylindrical or similarly shaped bodies. The force points are in good balance and symmetry. The stable and vigorous figures are shaped like bronze bells and they have strong cohesion inside. What the sculptor emphasize is the beauty of power embodied in bodies. This differs from the beauty of curves and flesh, which is attached great attention to in the western sculpture. Most of the pottery figures are in good proportion and degree of intensity and their structures are reasonable. This meets the requirement of plastic arts and reveal harmony and beauty to the public.

The moulds fuse appearance and qualities. The warriors standing like steel towers are boorish, straightforward and full of valour. The delicate warriors are elegant, bright and clever. The spirit is hidden in the body and the spirit becomes superficial when the body is well shaped. This is a rule of ancient Chinese plastic arts.

Bodies of the pottery figures are made in a simple and bright manner withont excessive ornaments. What they pursue is only the similarity in appearance. Nevertheless, heads are carved exquisitely and artistically exaggerated and refined skills are applied in the sculpture of key parts. For instance, eyebrows seem having no thickness. If eyebrows and superciliary ridges of pottery figures are carved like real ones, their faces are a little flat. Observed near, they are acceptable, but they get obscure and vague when people watch them from far. Therefore, pottery figures' eyebrows are exaggerated and thickness is added. As to their superciliary ridges, they have corners and edges. standing near these figures, people think they are similar to real ones in appearance. From the distance, people can see their facial organs clearly. Generally moustache is carred as if its roots come out of the skin to express the reality. As a matter of fact, moustache can by no means be seperated from faces. However. moustuche of the pottery figures is flying, standing or curred. The exaggeration doesn't make people feel that it is false. On the contrary, their characters become more distinct and outstanding.

Art presented in the Qin figures is colorful because it shapes varions kinds of typical characters. Take pottery generals for example, some long – beared generals, are dignified and steady and refined. Moustache of some generals looks like three drops of water and rouse up. They have bright piercing eyes and they are boorish. Honest faces of other generals imply their straightforward and unsophisticated nature. The outlook of ordinary warriors is even more changeable and variable, warriors of different ages have different beatings. For example, young warrior's faces are millow and full. They have smiling eyes and they are naive, innocent and lively. Older warriors with wrinkles on their foreheads are sedate and steady. warriors from different areas or of different nationalities do not look the same, either. Most warriors from Guan Zhong (in present shanxi province) usually have square or rectangular faces. Their features are rough and their temperament is straightforward. those from minority areas in northwest have projecting chins and their foreheads shrink back a little. some have whiskers and they are intrepid and valiant.

The Qin figures rise to a new state in the ancient sculpture history of China. They signify that the ancient sculpture is developing to its maturity and has formed the artistic style of Chinese character artistic style.

Making techniques of the pottery figures.

Pottery horses and warriors are all made by hand of clay, which is the mixture of local loess and appropriate amount of quartz sand. The loess to be washed and the impurity inside has to be removed before it ready. The making production includes three steps. First clay is shaped. After getting dried in a shadow, it is put into a pit and burnt. Finally the whole figure is colored.

Making pottery warriors: The body is progressively carved from bottom to top. That is to say, first make a square treadle. Next pile clay on the treadle and shape it into feet and legs. Then twine branches and cover them with clay to make a hollow body. After that, stick arms to the two sides of the body. The head and hands are made separately and then form an integrity together with other parts of the body. The outline of the head is made in a mould. Then variable facial features and expressions are carved more carefully. with regard to the making of pottery horses, first make the head, neck, trunk, limbs, tail and ears separately. Then stick them together to get the rudimentary sketch. Next cover the sketch with clay and carve it to the intended shape. The making of pottery horses and warriors grasps successfully the entire effect and combines organically sculpture, relief and line carving. The skills of carving, piling, kneading, sticking, sculpting, painting and so on are also applied to present the stereoscopic figure's posture, weight, appearance, expression, color, texture and other artistic effects.

Well − shaped pottery horses and warriors are burnt in pits and get finalized at about 950 to 1050 centigrade. The color is pure and the quality is hard. When knocked, they sounds rhythmic and sonorous. All these indicate that the technique of burning has risen to quite a high level at that time.

The whole bodies of pottery horses and warriors are colored after taken out of pits.

Made from mineral materials. The color includes red, pink, dark green, pinkish green, pinkish purple, sky blue, yellow, black, white and reddish brown. The way to color pottery figures is to spread raw paint on their bodies first and make them colorful next. Fundamentally, the color is bright and gorgeous, which makes the whole battle formation energetic, mighty and magnificent.

During the course of sorting and repairing the pottery horses and warriors, we find names of makers at some hidden corners on their bodies. By now we have discovered 87 different names. Some of them come from the central ceramic workshops, such as "Gong Qiang"、"Gong De"、"Gong Tin"、"Gong Chao"、"Gong Xi"、"Gong Po" etc. Others are from local personal ceramic workshops, such as "Xian Yang Fu"、"Xian Yang Yi""Xian Yang Jing"、"Li Jing Lian"、"Li Yang Chong". "An Yi Shu "and so on. The two groups of workers come from different areas and learn from different masters. Moreover, their respective experience and what they learn from real life are not the same. Therefore, each of them create artistic images of their specific style. On the whole, most figures made by workers from the central workshops are strong, powerful and full of vigour. They look like warriors guarding the gate of the palace. Also these workers are more skilled. Producfs of folk makers are pure, fresh and vary a lot in their appearance. Meanwhile, their skills are on uneven levels. The image, thought, emotion and characters of these pottery figures are more extensive, profound and socially representative.

Those who leave their names on pottery horses and warriors are all skilled technicians. Under their leadership, there are a good many workers who can not leave their names. If each technician has 10 apprentices, 87 technicians command 870 apprentices. In the sculpture history of the whole world, it is rare to find such a large team working together. These workers are creators of the Qin ceramic arts. Their names should be listed on a brilliant page in sculpture history of china and the whole world.

4. Weapons unearthed from the vaults

A large number of practical weapons unearthed from Pit 1, 2 and 3 can be generally classified into three categories: short weapons, long weapons, long − range weapons. Bronze swords and crescent goldenhooks belong to short weapons. In long weapons, there are the *Ge* (dagger − axe), *mao* (pikes), *ji* (halberds), *Shu*, *Yue* and other bronze weapons with long handles. Long − range weapons include bows, crossbows and a lot of bronze arrowheads. These pottery weapons are similar to those of one kind used in the middle and end of the warring states period. However, the following two kinds of special weapons are rarely seen.

Golden hooks: There are only two bronze golden hooks shaped like curved knives. They are made up of the body and the handle. The body is crescent with blades on two sides and the handle is elliptic cylindrical. The whole hook is 65.2 centimeters long and 2.2 to 3.5 centimeters wide. The weapon is found in archaeological history for the first time. The golden hooks were invented by the Wu people at the end of 6th century B.C. In 《The chronicle of Wu and Yue》, there are following lines: "Wu emperor informed his people, Those who are good at playing the hooks will get one hundred liang gold." The excessive Wu people began to make hooks. The two hooks are discovered beside officers at the left and right end of the vanguard in vault 1. They are ritual weapons, worn by the officers.

Long *bo*: Sixteen complete long bo were unearthed from Pit 1. As stabbing weapons with long handles, they are similar to pikes. The head of the long bo is shaped like daggers and it is installed at the top of the handle. Altogether it is 38 meters long. The blade is really sharp and it is a poverful antipersonnel weapon. The complete long bo has not been discovered before, so people only have vague impression of it and their ideas about its shape vary a lot. The long bo unearthed in the vault leads people out of the puzzle and gives them a clear idea.

All weapons unearthed Pit 1, 2 and 3 are made of bronze, which is the alloy of copper and tin. After shaped through casting, they are carefully filed and polished. When unearthed, the bronze sword hadn't be come rusty at all and it is as bright as the new one. After checking it, people find that the surface has been oxidized with chromium, which is antiseptic and rustproof. In the past, people believed that the technique of oxidization with chromium appeared in the 1930. Nevertheless, the technique was already invented in Qin Dynasty over 2000 years ago in China. This is regarded as a wonder in metallurgical history.

Blades of bronze swords、bo dagger－axes and pikes are all filed. Parallel, not crossing veins indicate that they are not filed by hand but some kind of simple filing machines. Surface of the weapons mentioned above are all polished and the smooth finish is between 6 and 8. This presents that technology used in processing metals has reached a fairly high level at that time. On the two sides of bronze bo, there are irregular designs like flames. The designs are neither casted nor carved. In stead, they merge in the surface and form an integrity with the superficial pattern. Some people believe the designs result from vulcanization.

There are two weapon − making systems in Qin Dynasty. One is central and the other is local. According to the inscription on weapons unearthed from the pits, they are all made by central official establishments. The weapons are of excellent quality and the technology applied in the making process is advanced. This is the peak in the production of bronze weapons in China.

5. The Terra − cotta Army and Qin Shihuang's Tomb

As a series of sacrificial vaults in Qin Shihuang's cemetery, the Terra − cotta Army is closely connected with the mausoleum. In ancient China, People traditionally believed that soul did not die after the body died. Instead, it lived in a gloomy world in the same way as if the body was alive. Therefore people should treat the dead's funeral and alive people equally. After their death, they still should own everything that they had when they were alive. Before he died, Qin Shihuang was an emperor. As a matter of fact, the archetectural structure of the cemetery and sacrificial objects are all designed and prepared based on the royal principle of ceremony and propriety.

Ever since the pits were discovered in 1974, we have systematically investigated and explored Qin Shihuang's mauoleum. Basically we know clear about the archetectural pattern of the funeral park now. Qin Shihuang's tomb is a square conical contour with a flat roof. At first it was 115 meters high and the bottom is 2000 meters in circumference. After over 2000 years of erosion by wind and rain as well as man's damage, now the tomb is 76 meters high and the perimeter at the bottom is 1390 meters. Around the tomb there are three circles of walls. Surrounding the underground palace, the wall of brick bases in the most interior is 4 meters high, 4 meters thick and 1704 meters in girth. The other two walls are on the ground and made of rammed clay. The one inside is 3870 meters in circumference and the one outside is 6210 meters. Doors are in four sides of the rectangular walls and on the top of doors there are watchtowers. This reveals that the archetectural pattern of Qin Shihuang's cemetery is the imitation of his capital.

Besides pits of the Terra − cotta Army, more than 200 pits of bronze chariots, stables, rare birds and animals and other sacrificial objects are also discovered in the cemetery. The pit of bronze chariots is quite large and the area is 3025 square meters. In

November 1980, part of the pit was tentatively excavated and people unearthed two great colored bronze chariots, which are half of the real ones in size. Made up of over 3000 parts, each chariot weighs more than 1000 kilograms. Both the horses and chariots with colored designs on are made of bronze and they have plenty of golden and silver ornaments. Among the chariots and horses discovered in archaeological history, the two have the highest rank, the most gorgeous decorations and the best preservation. Though both the two chariots have two wheels, one shaft and four horses harnessing in the front. They are different in their external forms. In the horizontal rectangular carriage of chariot 1, there is a high copper umbrella, under which stands a pottery driver. Bronze shields, crossbows and arrowheads are also discovered on the chariot. Chariot 2 has a closed carriage similar to a car. On the top of the carriage there is an oval cover. Windows are in the front, left and right sides of the carriage and a door is in the back. The door and windows can be opened and closed freely. The carriage is divided into the front and back part. In the front there is a kneeling driver and the owner of the chariot is in the back. Chariot 1 is for warriors and it was named "standing chariot" or "high chariot" in old times. Chariot 2, as a "luxury" one, has the door and windows. It is cool when the windows are open and warm when they are closed. Therefore it is also named "warm – cool chariot".

A guard of honour made up of chariots and horses is necessary when the emperor travelled. The guard of honour has three norms. The highest includes 81 chariots. There are 36 chariots in the middle and 9 chariots in the lowest. The two bronze chariots mentioned above belong to the middle insignia. In the team, chariot 1 is used to clear the way and protect other chariots, while chariot 2 is supplementary (also named "preparational chariot"). In 218 BC, Qin Shihuang travelled to the east. When he arrived at Bolangsha (in present Yangwu county He Nan Province), a strong man tried to assasinate Qin with a big steel mace, but he mistook the supplementary chariot for Emperor Qin's and Qin escaped the narrow death. However the emperor can also sit in the supplementary chariot. For instance, in 210 BC, on his way to the east, Qin Shihuang died in Sha Qiu (in present Guang Zhong County, He Bei Province). The body was carried back to Xian Yang in a luxury chariot. As models of Qin Shihuang's real chariots and horses, Chariot 1 and 2 were buried with the dead so that the emperor could use them when his soul travelled in the gloomy world.

In Qin Shihuang's cemetery, one pit of a large stable and 98 pits of small stables are also discovered. Abont 500 horses in these pits are all real ones, some are alive when buried and some are killed first then buried. Before the horses' heads are pottery basins with grains and grass in and pots with water in. They represent horses' trough. The 1.9 – meter – tall warriors in the large stable and the kneeling ones in small stables are stockmen. On the ceramics unearthed in vaults of stables, there are names of stables, such as "Big stable", "small stable", "Palace Stable", "Middle Stable" and "Left Stable". In Qin Shihuang's time, there were many places raising horses inside and outside the capital because lots of them were needed to draw chariots and serve in the cavalry. After Qin's death, a large number of horses were buried underground to work for his soul.

When alive, Qin Shihuang also liked hunting, so in his cemetery, many pits of rare birds and animals were built. By now one such pit has been discovered.

There are too many sacrificial pits discovered in Qin Shihuang's cemetery to list one by one. In short, in his cemetery, Qin Shihuang builteverything that he had in his life. The underground kingdom is a copy of the one on the ground. Lots of warriors guarded Qin Shihuang's capital, Xian Yang when he was alive. After his death, 8000 pottery warriors and horses were buried with him to guard his unified country and defend the emperor's paramount dignity.

Qin Shihuang's mausoleum is a treasure – house of relics. With the further development of archaeological exploration, more new relics will be continually discovered. Some archaeologists said humorously: "Qin Shihuang's cemetery is a famons travelling resort and archoeologists' heaven". These words are really true.

The Terra – cotta Army Museum
November 8.1998.

Content

1. The view of Qin Shihuang's cemetery
(Northeast – Southwest)

2. The view of Qin Shihuang's cemetery

3. The Pit 1 exhibition hall

4. The Pit 1

5. The rear view of Pit 1

7. The Excavation of pottery horses and warriors in Pit 1

5. The Excavation of pottery horses and warriors in Pit 1

8. The Excavation of kneeling warriors in Pit 2

The Excavation
kneeling warriors
Pit 2

10. The partial battle formation in Pit 1 (Southeast – Northwest)

11. The warrior formation in Pit 1 (rear view)

12. The warrior formation in Pit 1

13. The warrior formation in Pit 1

17   14. The warrior formation in Pit 1

15. The warrior formation in Pit 1

16. The warrior formation in Pit 1

17. The warrior formation in Pit

18. The warriors in Pit 1

19. The warrior formation in Pit 1

20. The warriors in Pit 1

1. The formation
f pottery warriors
nd horses in Pit 1

22. The formation of pottery horses and warriors in Pit 1

23. Pottery horses in the east of Pit 1

24. The Pit 3

25. Pottery horses and warriors in Pit 3

26. The rear view of a pottery general 30
(unearthed in Pit 1)

7. Pottery general
(unearthed in Pit 1)

28. The back view of
a pottery general
(unearthed in Pit 2)

29. Pottery general
(unearthed in Pit 2)

30. Pottery general
(unearthed in Pit 1)

31. Medium – ranking officer
(unearthed in Pit 1)

33. The back view of a medium – ranking officer (unearthed in Pit 3)

32. Medium – ranking officer (unearthed in Pit 1)

34. Part of a
pottery driver
(unearthed in
Pit 2)

35. Chariot Right
(unearthed in Pit 2)

36. Chariot Left
(unearthed in Pit 2)

37. Cavalrymen (unearthed in Pit 2)

38. Standing warrior
(unearthed in Pit 2)

39. Standing warrior
(unearthed in Pit 2)

41. Kneeling warrior
(unearthed in Pit 2)

40. Cavalrymen
(unearthed in Pit 2)

42. Kneeling warrior (unearthed in Pit 2)
43. The back view of kneeling warrior.
44. Kneeling warrior.

45. Kneeling warrior (unearthed in Pit 2)
46. Kneeling warrior

48

47. Armoured warrior
(unearthed in Pit 1)

48. Armoured
warrior
(unearthed in
Pit 1)

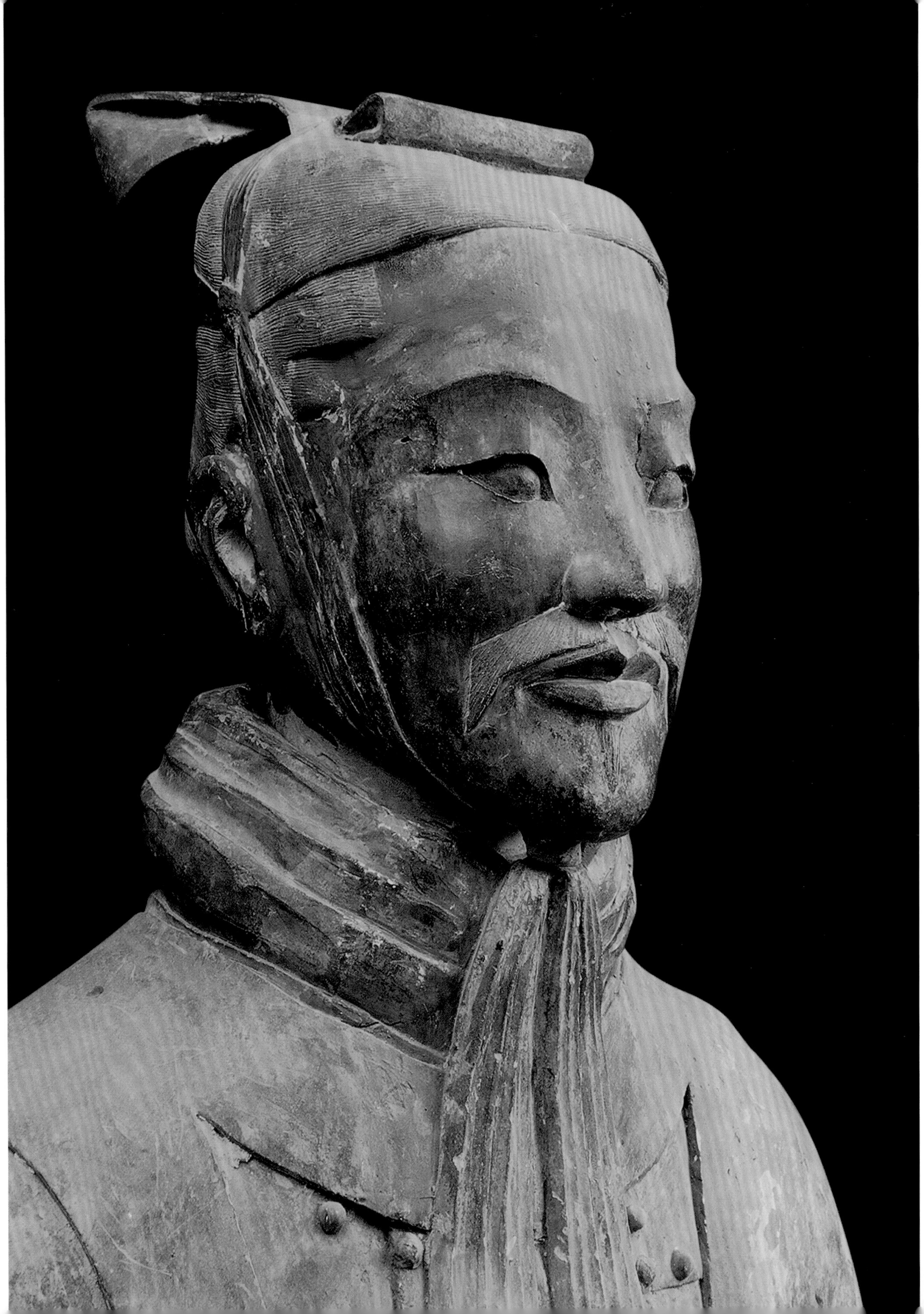

9. The head
f a medium-
anking officer
unearthed in
it 2)

50. The head of a warrior. (unearthed in Pit 1)

51. The head of a warrior. (unearthed in Pit 1)

52. The head of
a warrior.
(unearthed in Pit 2)

53. The head of a warrior. (unearthed in Pit 2)   54. The head of a warrior. (unearthed in Pit 1)

55. The head of a warrior. (unearthed in Pit 1)

56. The head of a warrior. (unearthed in Pit 1)

57. The head of a warrior. (unearthed in Pit 1)

58. The head of a warrior. (unearthed in Pit 1)

59. The head of a warrior.
(unearthed in Pit 2)

60. The head of
a warrior.
(unearthed in
Pit 2)

61. The head of
a warrior.
(unearthed in Pit 1)

62. The head of a warrior. (unearthed in Pit 1)   63. The head of a warrior. (unearthed in Pit 1)

4. The head of
warrior.
unearthed in Pit 1)

65. The head of a warrior. (unearthed in Pit 1)　　66. The head of a warrior. (unearthed in Pit 1)

67. The head of a warrior. (unearthed in Pit 1)

68. The head of a warrior. (unearthed in Pit 1)

73. The head of
a general
(unearthed in Pit 1)

69. The head of
a warrior.
(unearthed in Pit 1)
70. The head of
a warrior
(unearthed in Pit 1)
71. The head of
a warrior
(unearthed in Pit 1)
72. The head of
a warrior
(unearthed in Pit 1)

74. The head of a warrior (unearthed in Pit 1)

75. The head of a warrior (unearthed in Pit 1)

The head of
warrior
nearthed in Pit 1)

77. The head of a warrior (unearthed in Pit 1)

78. The head of a warrior (unearthed in Pit 1)

79. The head of a warrior (unearthed in Pit 1)

80. The head of a warrior (unearthed in Pit 1)

81. The head
an officer
(unearthed in
Pit 1)

82. The head of
an officer
(unearthed in Pit
1)

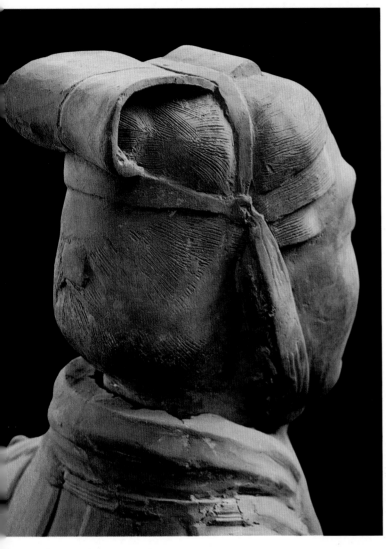

83. The hair style of an officer (unearthed in Pit 1)

84. The hair style of an officer (unearthed in Pit 2)

85. The hair style of a general (unearthed in Pit 1)

86. The hair style of an officer (unearthed in Pit 3)

87. The hair style of a warrior (unearthed in Pit 1)

88. The hair style of a warrior (unearthed in Pit 1)

74

89. The hair style of a warrior (unearthed in Pit 1)　　90. The hair style of a warrior (unearthed in Pit 2)

75

91. Warriors' short boots (unearthed in Pit 1)

92. Soles of kneeling warriors' boots (unearthed in Pit 2)

3. Warriors'
hooks
unearthed
(in Pit 1)

4. Warriors'
hooks
unearthed
(in Pit 1)

95. Warriors' hook
(unearthed in Pit 1)
96. Warriors' hook
(unearthed in Pit 1)
97. Warriors' hook
(unearthed in Pit 1)

98. The colored head of a warrior (unearthed in Pit 1)

99. The colored head of a warrior (unearthed in Pit 1)　　　100. The colored head of a warrior (unearthed in Pit 1)

101. The colored design on a general's armor (unearthed in Pit 1)
102. The colored design on a general's armor (unearthed in Pit 1)

104. A bronze bo
with inscription
(unearthed in Pit 1)
105. A bronze bo
with inscription
(unearthed in Pit 1)

103. A bronze sword
(unearthed in Pit 1)

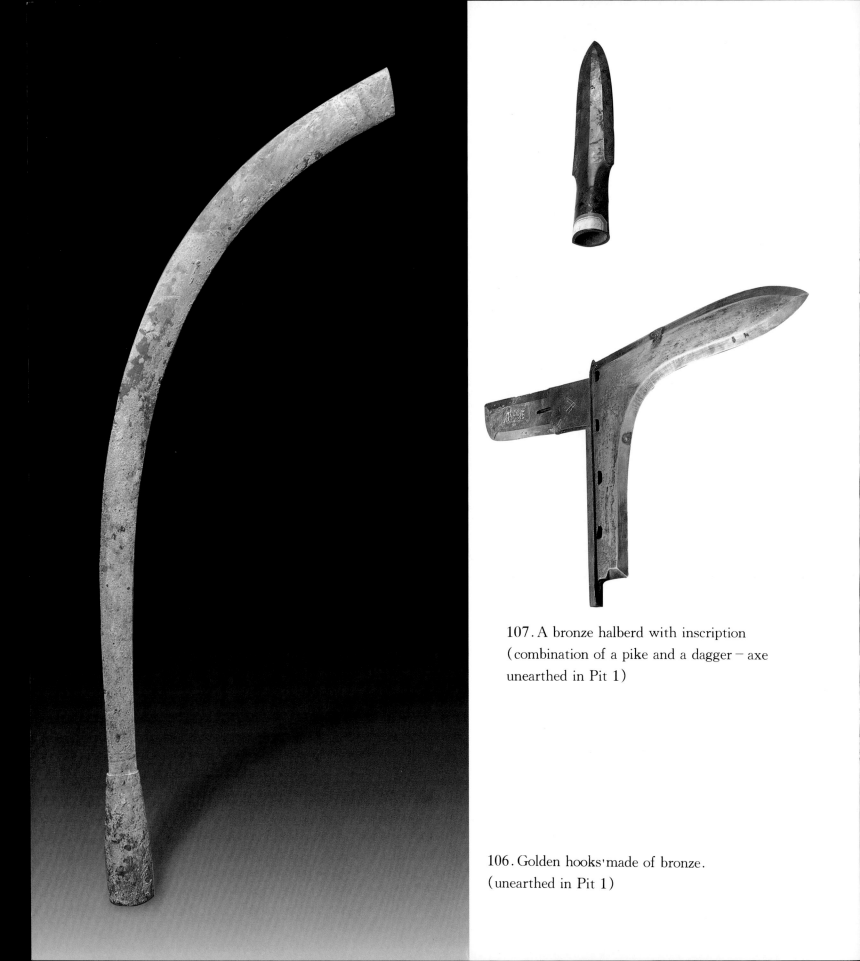

107. A bronze halberd with inscription
(combination of a pike and a dagger – axe
unearthed in Pit 1)

106. Golden hooks made of bronze.
(unearthed in Pit 1)

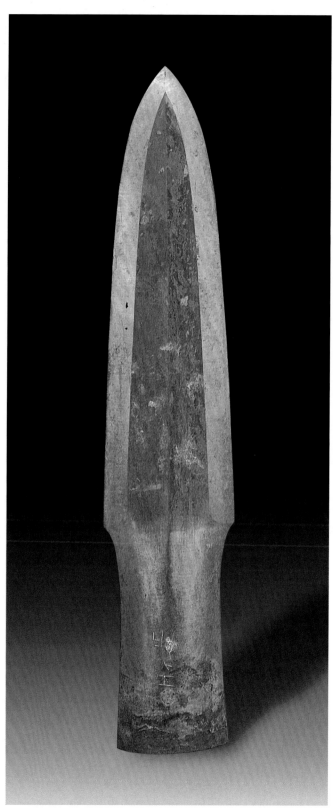

108. A bronze pike with inscription
(unearthed in Pit 1)

109. A bronze pike with inscription
(unearthed in Pit 1)

110. The unearthing of bronze chariots (east to west)

111. The original expression of Chariot 1.

112. The Cleaning in
the excavation site of
bronze chariots
113. The restoring
site of Chariot 1

114. The rebuilt Bronze chariots

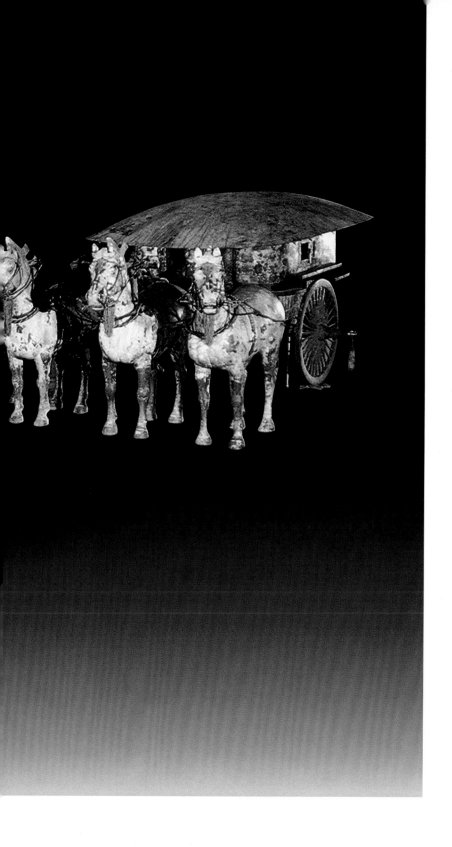

115. Bronze Chariot 1

116. Part of bronze Chariot 1

117. The charioteer
on Chariot 1

121. The shaft, horizontal log and yoke of chariots

122. Silver and gold headstall with bit ▶

123. Gold – inlaid silver
canopy stick on Chariot 1

124. The canopy above Chariot 1
125. Wheels of the bronze chariot

126. The carriage
of Chariot 1.
127. The interior of t
carriage of chariot 1

128. The silver and gold necklace of the bronze horse.
129. The cover of Chariot 2

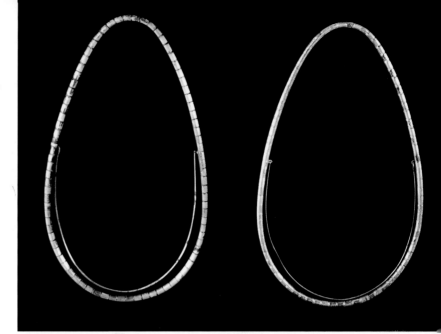

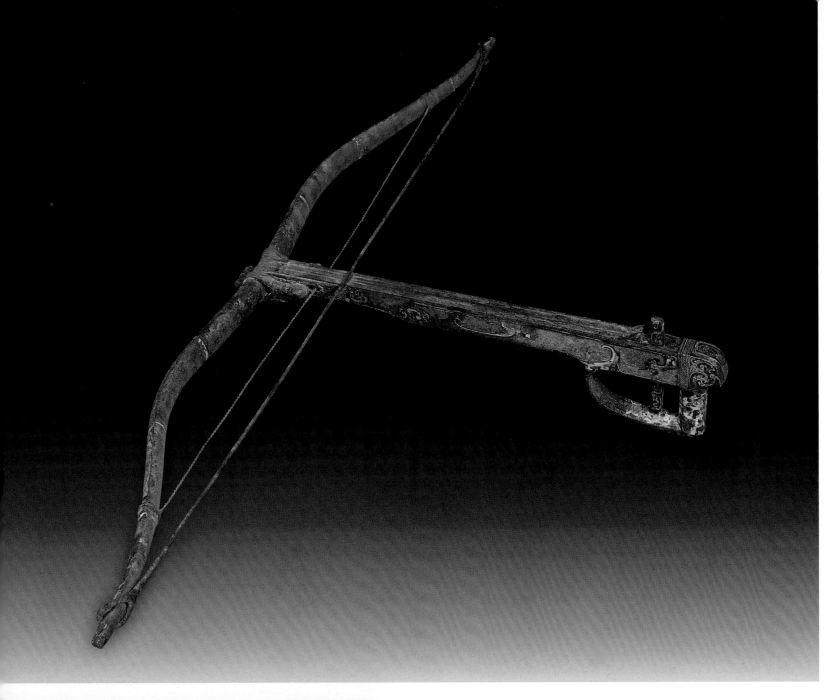

130. The bronze crossbow on Chariot 1
131. Part of the bronze crossbow

132. The silver crossbow on Chariot 1.
133. The bronze shield on Chariot 1

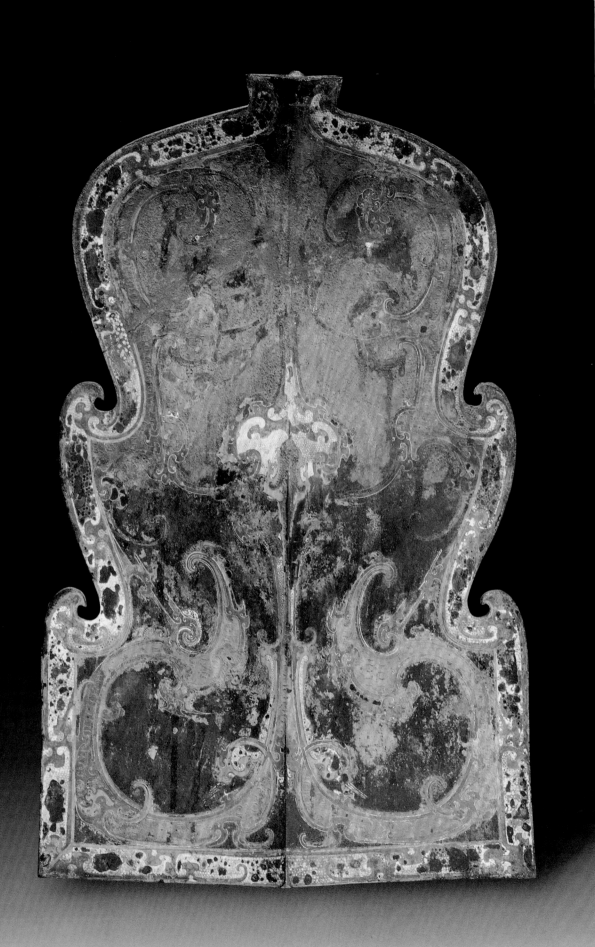

134. The bronze
shield
135. Back of the
bronze shield

136. The bronze arrow container and arrows on chariot 1

137. The colored
design on the arrow
container.

138. The colored
design on the arrow
container.

139. The colored
design on the door
of Chariot 2

140. The colored design on the front board of Chariot 1

142. The bronze rectangular
pot on Chariot 1 (lid removed)

141. The bronze rectangular pot on Chariot 1

143. Pottery stockmen
(unearthed in the Pit of
stables that looks like a
carpenter's square
in Qin Shi huang's cemetery)

144. Pottery stockmen
(unearthed in the Pit
of stables that looks like a
carpenter's square in
Qin Shihuang's cemetery)

145. Kneeling
stockman's head.
（unearthed in the small
Pit of stables in
Qin Shi huang's
cemetery）

46. Kneeling
tockman's head.
unearthed in the small
'it of stables in
)in Shihuang's
emetery)

111

147. Kneeling stockman (unearthed in the small Pit of stables in Qin Shi huang's cemetery)

8. Kneeling stockman
unearthed in the small
of stables in
n Shihuang's
netery)

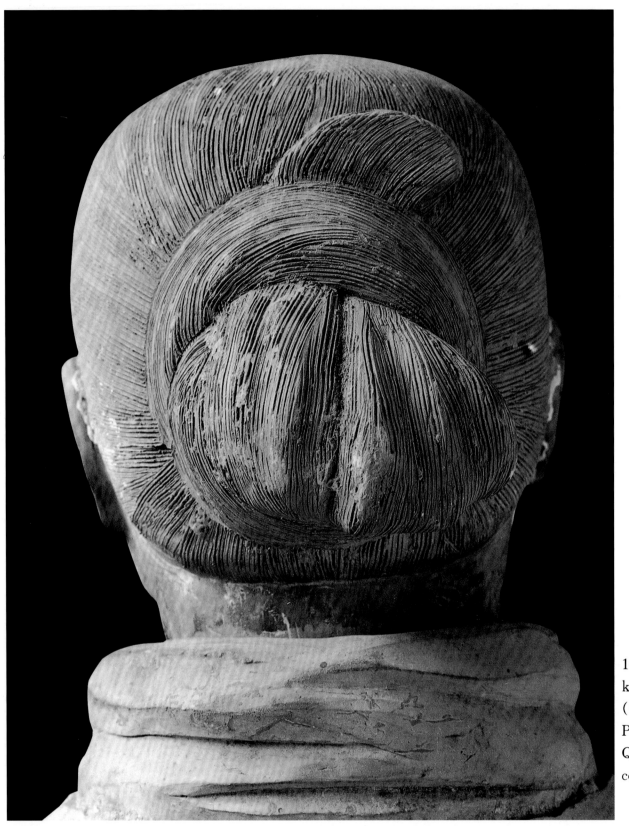

149. The hair style of
kneeling stockman
(unearthed in the sma[ll]
Pit of stables in
Qin Shi huang's
cemetery)

150. The head of a
kneeling stockman
(unearthed in the small
Pit of stables in
Qin Shihuang's
cemetery)

151. The gold – inlaid silver bronze bell of a musical establishment(unearthed in Qin Shihuang's cemetery)

Photographer：Xia Juxian
Front cover designer：Zhang Xiguang
Executive editor：Sun Yarong
Layout designer：Liang Ye
Executive Printer：Zhang Daoqi
Executive Proofreader：Zhang Yang

图书在版编目（CIP）数据

秦始皇陵兵马俑：英文/秦始皇兵马俑博物馆编．

北京：文物出版社，1999.9

ISBN 7－5010－1155－9

Ⅰ．秦…　Ⅱ．秦…　Ⅲ．秦始皇陵-兵马俑-图录　Ⅳ．K878.9

中国版本图书馆 CIP 数据核字(1999)第 45603 号

The Terra-cotta Army in the Mausoleum of Qin Shihuang
_____

Edited by The Terra-cotta Army Museum
Published by Cultural Relics Publishing House
No. 29 Wusi Dajie
http://www.wenwu.com
E-mail：web@wenwu.com
Printed by He Bei No. 2 Xin Hua printing house
Distributed by Xin Hua Bookstore
_____

787×1092　1/12开　印张：12
First Printed in September, 1999
Third printed in June, 2001
ISBN 7－5010－1155－9/K·467